Vocal Selections from

The Fantasticks

Lyrics by
TOM JONES

Music by
HARVEY SCHMIDT

T0052947

50th
Anniversary Edition

Alfred

Produced by
Alfred Music Publishing Co., Inc.
P.O. Box 10003
Van Nuys, CA 91410-0003
alfred.com

Printed in USA.

ISBN-10: 0-7390-7311-7
ISBN-13: 978-0-7390-7311-7

The facade of the Sullivan Street Playhouse, at 181 Sullivan Street in New York's Greenwich Village, where THE FANTASTICKS opened on May 3, 1960, and ran for 42 years.

(Photo: John Schak)

The Fantasticks at 50

The Fantasticks at 50

TOM JONES
Lyrics

I'm beginning to feel like the portrait of Dorian Gray. While I sit hidden at my desk, growing older and older, *The Fantasticks* continues running at the Jerry Orbach Theater in New York, as fresh and as young as ever.

Why has *The Fantasticks* run such a long time? That is a question composer Harvey Schmidt and I have often been asked over the years. Why has this seemingly simple romantic fable with the fetching score been able to survive so many cultural changes and be welcome in so many foreign lands? The answer, of course, lies partly in the score itself, the combination of catchy "show biz" tunes and unabashedly romantic ballads. But beyond that, there is something else, something more complicated. I'm not exactly sure what it is, but I do have some thoughts about it.

First of all, there is the fact that *The Fantasticks* may be taken on several different levels. Young children like it for the clown-like comedy. Teenagers (always our best audiences) like the Romeo and Juliet aspects. Parents identify with the parents. Theatre people enjoy the countless theatrical references. And some people, like the famed author and anthropologist Joseph Campbell, have seen in it the re-enactment of an ancient myth.

Using such time-honored theatrical devices as a narrator-chorus, spoken verse, direct address to the audience, stock characters from Commedia dell'Arte, and even the "invisible prop man" from the Oriental theatre, the show attempts to establish its own reality; a tacit agreement between the actors and the audience to create an imaginary world together, to draw forth moonlight from a cardboard disc, and by an act of mutual magic, to transform a few scraps of torn paper into gently falling snow. "On your imaginary forces work," says Shakespeare, and that precept has been our guide.

The Fantasticks is also an attempt to celebrate romanticism and to mock it at the same time. The most tender moments are suddenly and deliberately "cut" by laughter. Conversely, the funny moments are often meant to turn on themselves and become touching. It is this duality that helps to give *The Fantasticks* its distinctive tone and keeps it from being the simple "boy meets girl" story which it seems on the surface to be.

Whatever it is, it is. I am content to watch in awe as the show goes on, defying time, while I continue to ripen on the vine.

The Fantasticks at 50

HARVEY SCHMIDT

Music

I am pleased that this new edition of vocal selections from *The Fantasticks* contains three additional songs:

1. "This Plum Is Too Ripe"
In the show, this is a quartet for the two fathers and their children. It is re-imagined here as a jazzy solo.

2. "Metaphor"
This love song was originally written as a duet for the Boy and Girl.

3. "A Perfect Time to Be in Love"
I am especially pleased to include this piece, available in print for the first time. It was created expressly for Robert Goulet to sing as El Gallo in the fully-orchestrated 30th anniversary tour of the show. Around this period, we'd begun experimenting with writing songs based on a title, rather than a full lyric or completed melody, as a direct result of having read an interview with Lerner and Loewe, who wrote most of their songs this way. In doing so, neither collaborator feels overly restricted at the start of the process. So, having chosen to musicalize the moment just before the Boy and the Girl meet at night for the first time, we agreed on this title. I then built a melody around it and Tom completed the lyric. It came together quickly, fitting snugly into the score and providing El Gallo with a quiet moment to recall a similar time in his own youth.

During our 60-year partnership, however, we've used every method of composition: words first, music first, and sometimes working together at the piano. The songs in *The Fantasticks* reflect all those different approaches, but no matter the route, the goal is to have the song finally "feel right." Many years after creating this score, we find we still get pleasure from the work we did way back then, and having written some songs that continue being appreciated by performers and audiences all over the world is our ultimate reward. We hope this newly-expanded collection brings you some of that same enjoyment.

TRY TO REMEMBER

Lyrics by
TOM JONES

Music by
HARVEY SCHMIDT

Rather slowly (♩ = 126)

Keep pedal very light

Try to re-mem-ber the kind of Sep-tem-ber when life was slow and oh, so mel-low. Try to re-mem-ber the kind of Sep-tem-ber when grass was green and grain was

Try to Remember - 6 - 1

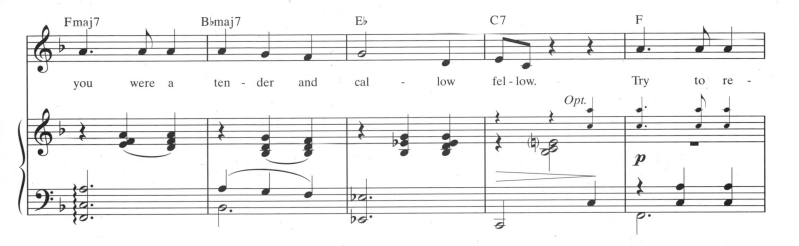

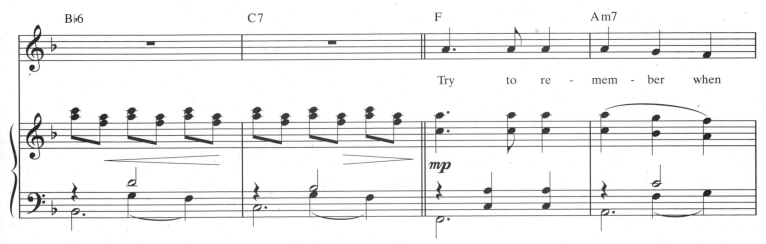

Try to Remember - 6 - 2

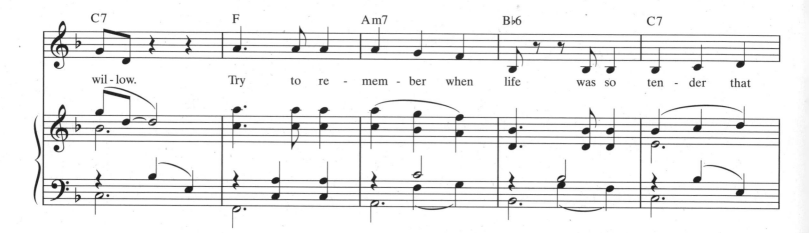

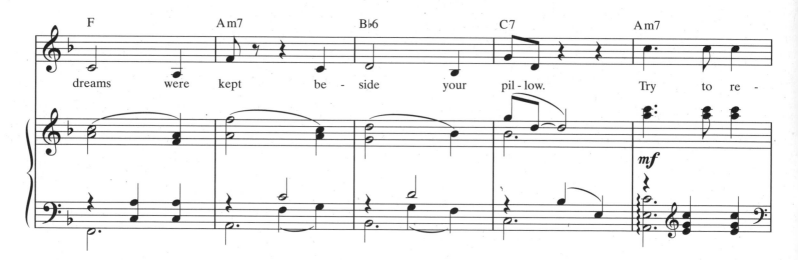

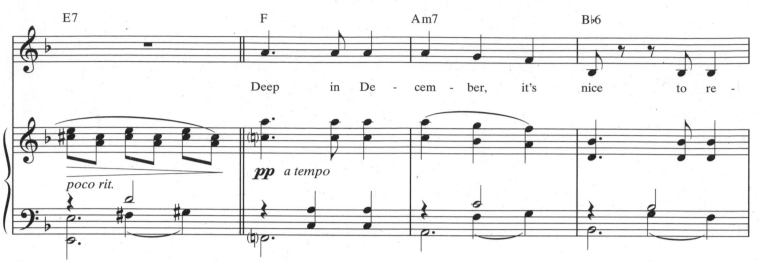

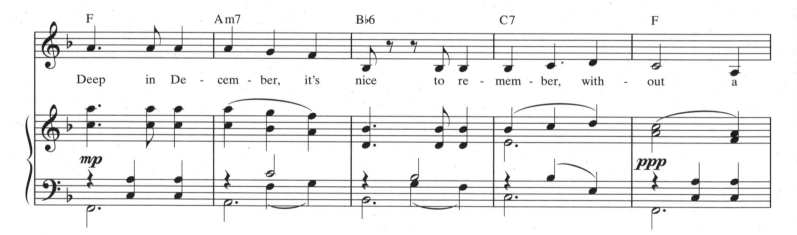

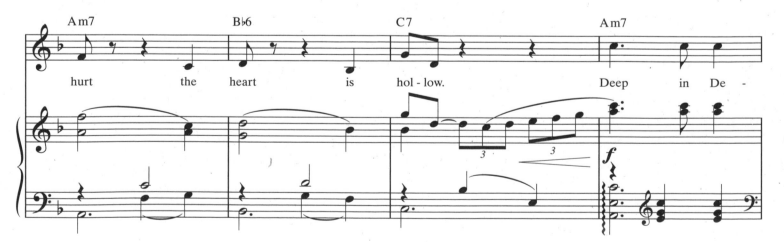

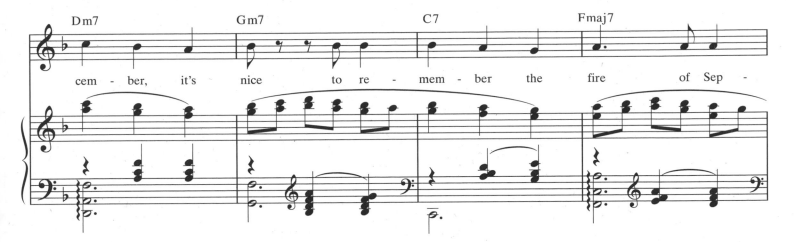

cem - ber, it's nice to re - mem - ber the fire of Sep -

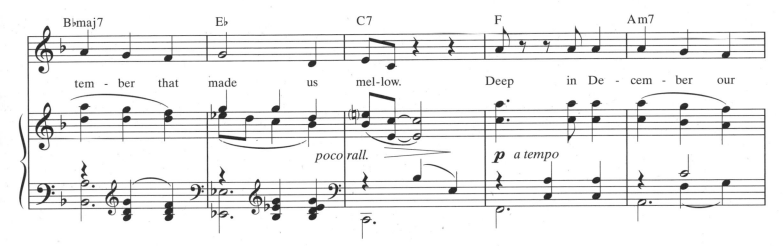

tem - ber that made us mel - low. Deep in De - cem - ber our

poco rall. *p* *a tempo*

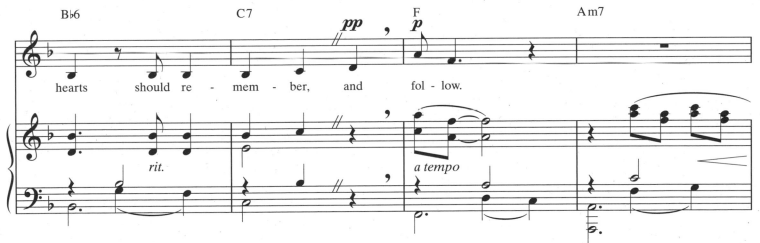

hearts should re - mem - ber, and fol - low.

rit. *a tempo*

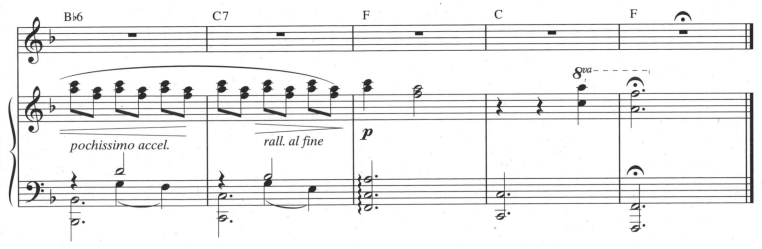

pochissimo accel. *rall. al fine* *p*

I CAN SEE IT

Lyrics by
TOM JONES

Music by
HARVEY SCHMIDT

Moderato

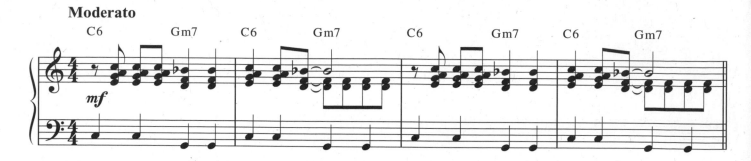

Refrain: (soft but rhythmically)

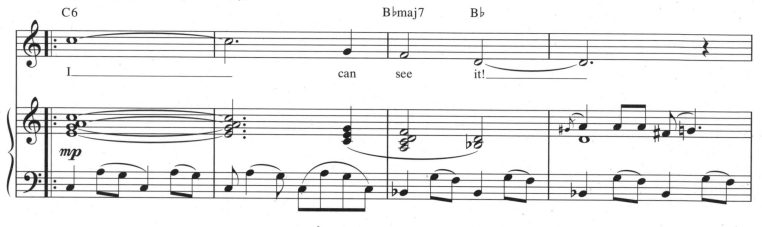

I_____ can see it!

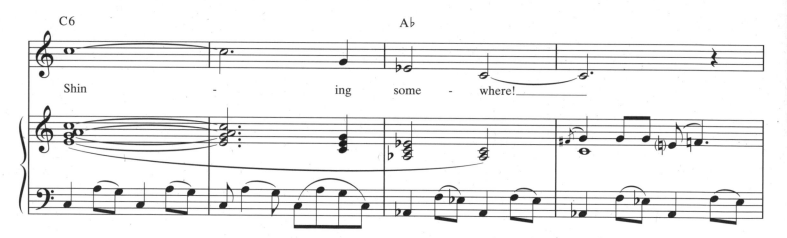

Shin - - - ing some - where!_____

Bright lights some - where in - vite___ me to come there_____ and

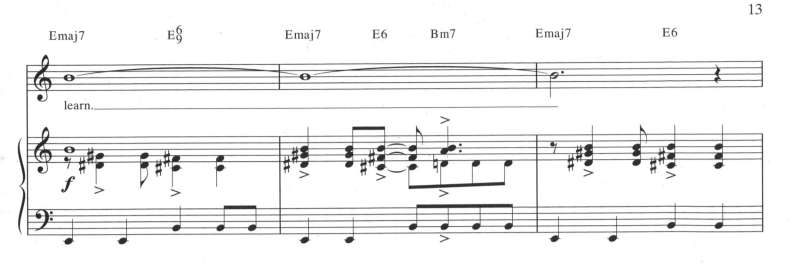

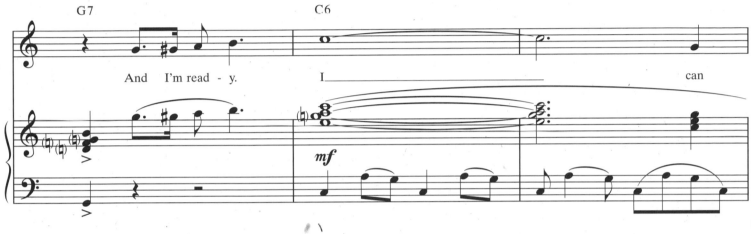

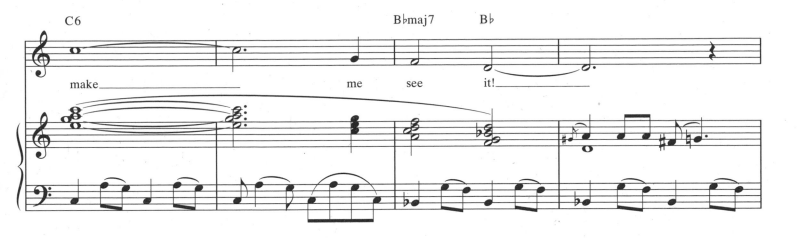

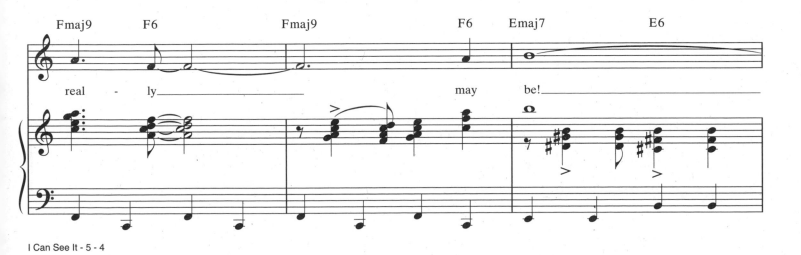

MUCH MORE

Lyrics by
TOM JONES

Music by
HARVEY SCHMIDT

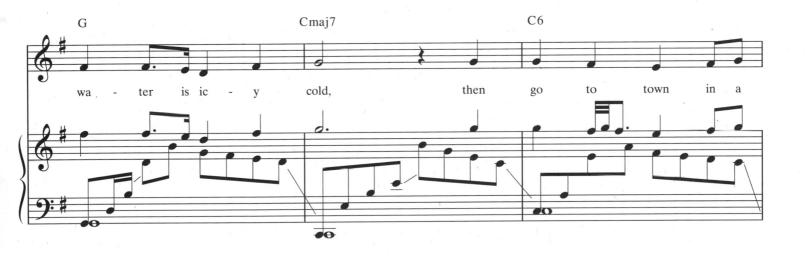

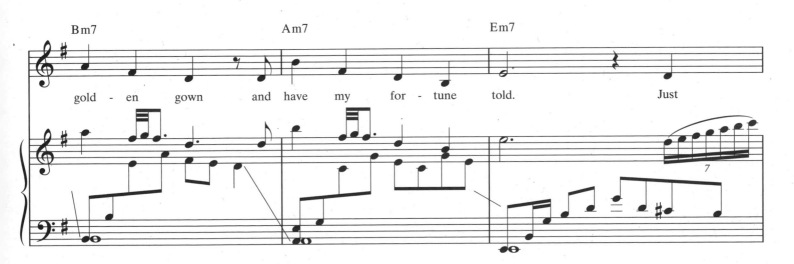

Much More - 5 - 1

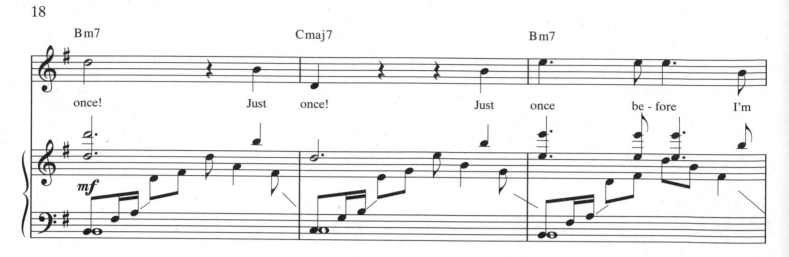

once! Just once! Just once be - fore I'm

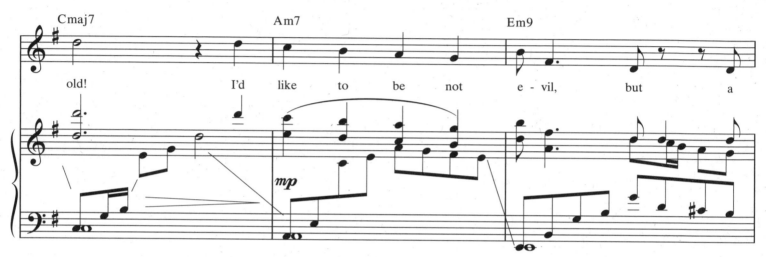

old! I'd like to be not e - vil, but a

lit - tle world - ly - wise; to be the kind of

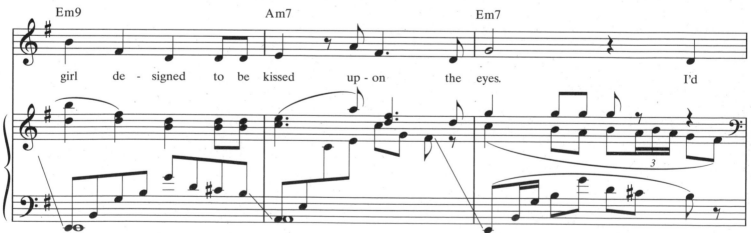

girl de - signed to be kissed up - on the eyes. I'd

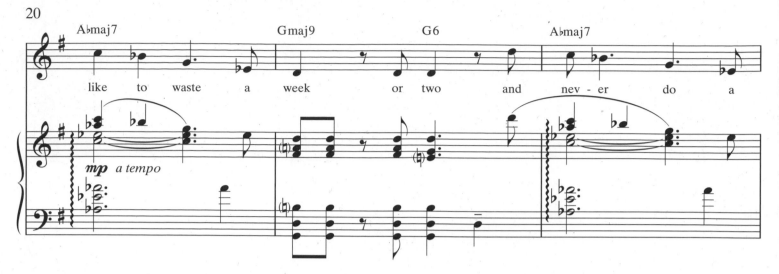

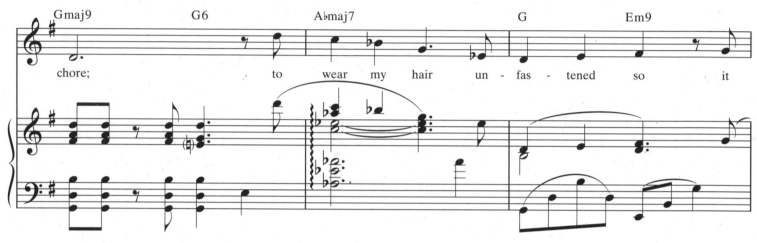

NEVER SAY NO

Lyrics by
TOM JONES

Music by
HARVEY SCHMIDT

Refrain: (moderately)

1. Dogs got to bark, a mule's got to bray, sol-diers must fight, and
2. Dogs got to bark, a mule's got to bray, sol-diers must fight, and

preach-ers must pray. And chil-dren, I guess, must get their own way the
preach-ers must pray. And chil-dren, I guess, must get their own way the

min-ute that you say "no." Why did the kids pour jam on the cat?
min-ute that you say "no." Why did the kids put beans in their ears?

Never Say No - 3 - 1

swim - min' ev - er since! / got a son - in - law! Ohhhh! Ohhhh!

Tempo I

Sure as a June comes right af - ter May, sure as the night comes right af - ter day,

you can be sure the dev - il's to pay the min - ute that you say "no."

Make sure you nev - er say "no!"

ERIK ALTEMUS as Matt and KIMBERLY WHALEN as Luisa,
at the Jerry Orbach Theater in New York City, 2010.
(Photo: Carol Rosegg)

Author TOM JONES as the Old Actor, a role he played in the original Sullivan Street production in 1960, and again (above) on the 50th Anniversary of the show in 2010, at the Jerry Orbach Theater. (Photo: Carol Rosegg)

Right: MARTIN VIDNOVIC as Bellomy, SANTINO FONTANA as Matt, SARA JEAN FORD as Luisa, and LEO BURMESTER as Hucklebee in the 2006 revival at the Jerry Orbach Theater. (Photo: Joan Marcus)

Left: SAL PROVENZA as El Gallo, JUDITH BLAZER as Luisa, and CHRISTOPHER SEPPE as Matt. Sullivan Street Playhouse. (Photo: Lou Manna)

LORE NOTO (the original producer) played the role of Hucklebee for 16 years in the Sullivan Street production, earning an award from the Guinness Book of World Records.

ROBERT GOULET as El Gallo, in the 30th Anniversary tour. (Photo: Neal Preston)

Left: LIZA MINNELLI as Luisa in a 1963 East Coast tour, directed by WORD BAKER, and co-starring ELLIOTT GOULD. (Photo: Ray Fisher)

The original Sullivan Street cast, beginning clockwise, with HUGH THOMAS (Bellomy) in straw hat, TOM JONES (Henry) in mask, BLAIR STAUFFER (Mute) in top hat, JERRY ORBACH (El Gallo) in sombrero, JAY HAMPTON (Handyman) in glasses, KENNETH NELSON (Matt) in sweater, WILLIAM LARSEN (Hucklebee) in suspenders, GEORGE CURLEY (Mortimer) in feather, and RITA GARDNER (Luisa) standing in the center.

(Photo: Robert Benton)

PLANT A RADISH

Lyrics by
TOM JONES

Music by
HARVEY SCHMIDT

Plant a Radish - 4 - 1

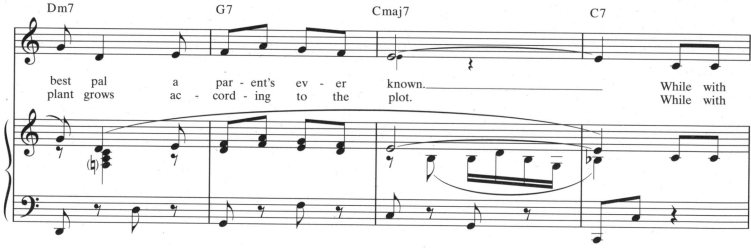

know un - til the seed is near - ly grown just what you've sown. So
soon as you think you know what kind you've got, it's what they're not. So

plant a car - rot, get a car - rot, not a brus - sel sprout.
plant a cab - bage, get a cab - bage, not a sau - er - kraut.

That's why I love veg - 'ta - bles; you know what you're a - bout!

Life is mer - ry if it's ver - y veg - e - tar - i - an. A

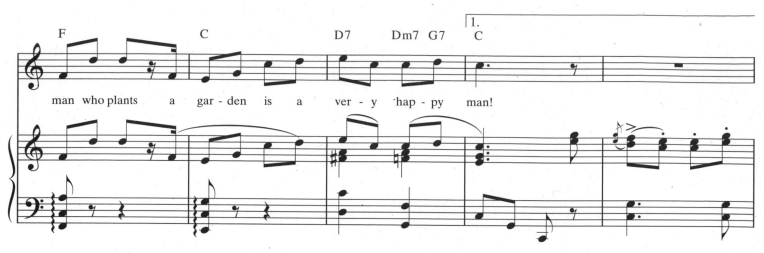

man who plants a gar-den is a ver-y hap-py man!

man! A veg-e-tar-i-

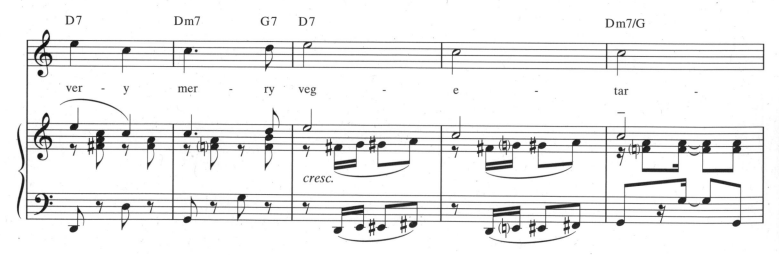

ver-y mer-ry veg - e - tar -

i - an.

SOON IT'S GONNA RAIN

Lyrics by
TOM JONES

Music by
HARVEY SCHMIDT

THEY WERE YOU

Lyrics by
TOM JONES

Music by
HARVEY SCHMIDT

THIS PLUM IS TOO RIPE

Lyrics by
TOM JONES

Music by
HARVEY SCHMIDT

Swing 4 with a jazz beat ♩ = 138 (♫ = ♩³♪)

Take a - way the gold - en moon-beam.
Take a - way the sense of dra - ma.

Take a - way the tin - sel sky.___ What at night seems
Take a - way the pup - pet play.___ What at night seems

This Plum Is Too Ripe - 4 - 1

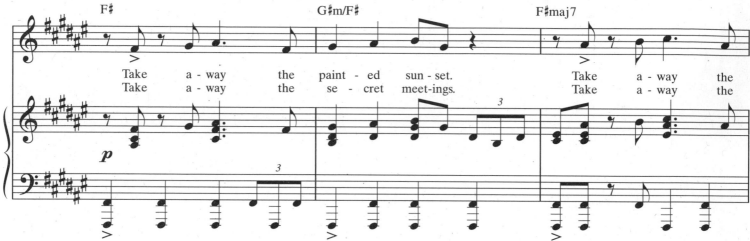

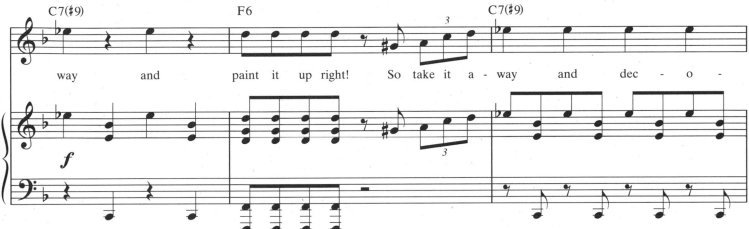

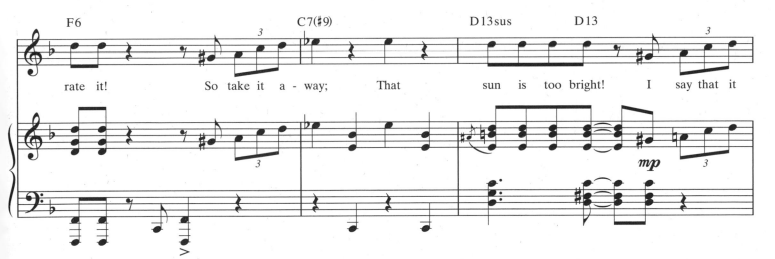

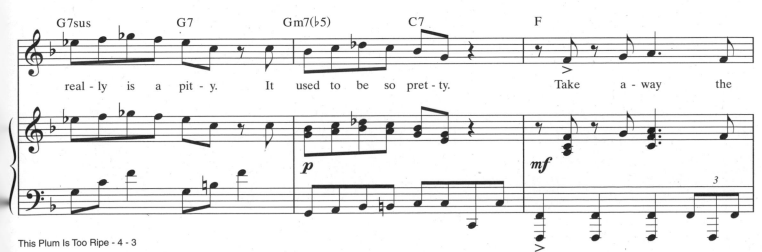

METAPHOR

Lyrics by
TOM JONES

Music by
HARVEY SCHMIDT

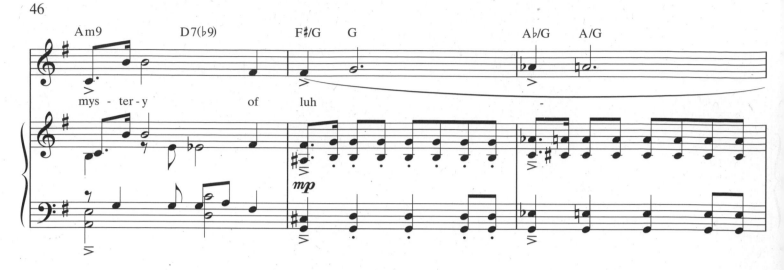

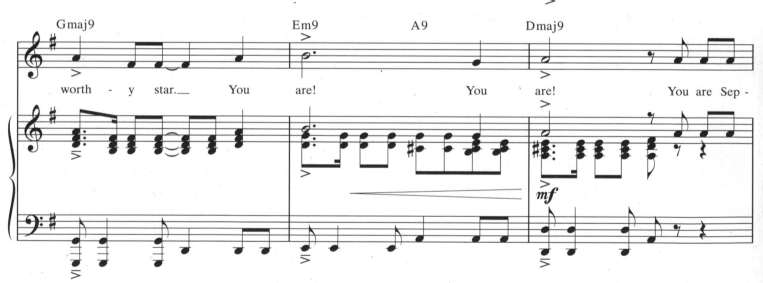

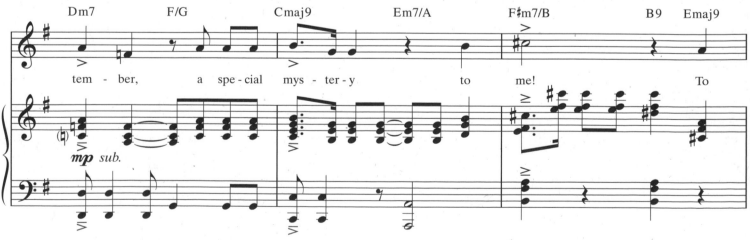

A PERFECT TIME TO BE IN LOVE

Lyrics by
TOM JONES

Music by
HARVEY SCHMIDT

A Perfect Time to Be in Love - 4 - 1

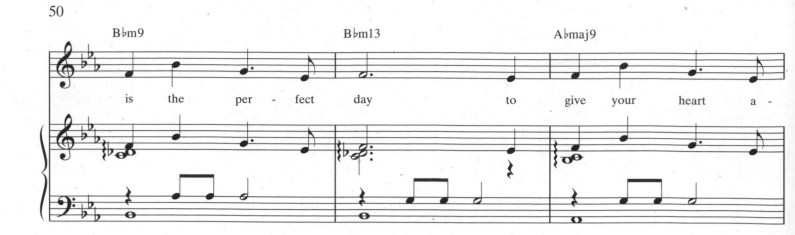

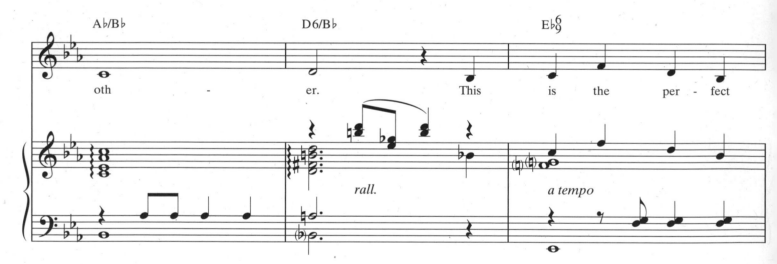

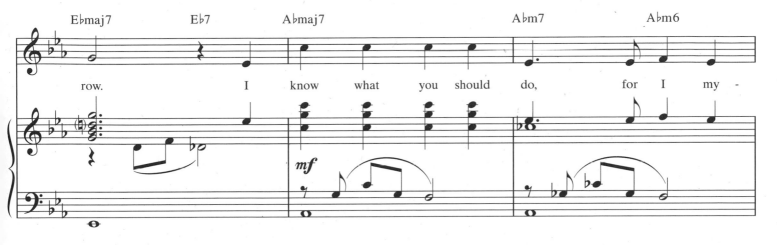

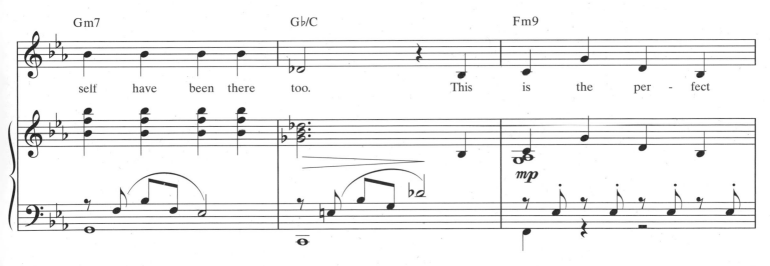

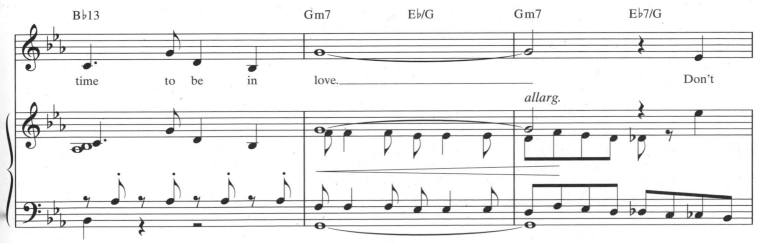